# QUEEN VICTORIA

University Press
Copyright © 2019

# Table of Contents

# Introduction

The Victorian Era is known as a time of straitlaced morals and sexual repression. During that time, the British people, particularly the middle classes, embraced strict moral standards. So, it stands to reason that Queen Victoria, Britain's Sovereign, and one of the most influential people at the time, would have had something to do with that.

Yet, it is often true that a famous person that stands behind a legend like this is nothing like the general perception of her. The question arises, what kind of person and what kind of ruler was Queen Victoria? Was she really a prude and a disciplinarian? Was she modest, quiet, and demure? A closer study of her life reveals something quite different.

Victoria was a prolific diary writer. Her writings exposed a side of her character that departs from the myth in nearly every sense. Why is it that the first thing people think of when they hear "Victorian" is blandness and coldness? Perhaps it is the image of short, pudgy Victoria herself that hides the fact that she was actually a woman filled with passion and inner fire.

Enormous changes in government and culture marked the Victorian Era. Britain went from obeying the wishes of a single monarch to making decisions for itself through a newer, more powerful Parliament and increased individual input into the political process.

Queen Victoria's relationships with the prime ministers of her country were, at times, productive and, at other times, filled with discord. Yet, the country enjoyed a long period of peace and stability during her reign. Somehow, she managed to unite the country at a time when opposing factions fought battles on the home front. Queen Victoria proved herself a great and influential Queen and helped to change the course of Britain's future forever.

# Chapter 1

## Race to the Throne

Before Princess Victoria Alexandrina was born, her father and his brothers were running a race that would change the course of life in the U.K. for decades and impact the entire future of the country. Yet, even with such high stakes involved, the runners had only a limited amount of control over the outcome. That is because the goal of the race was to be the first to produce an heir apparent for the throne of the British monarchy. If Prince Edward, Duke of Kent and Strathearn, had not won the competition, Victoria would never have been Queen.

The race started when the granddaughter and only heir of Prince Edward's brother, King George III, died in 1817. Her absence brought on a succession crisis in the U.K. His married brothers were out of the race for various reasons. The unmarried brothers had to get married and produce children quickly if they wanted one of their children to become the next

King or Queen. Whichever of the brothers had a child first to carry on the monarchy would not only win a place as the father of the monarch but would also gain a financial reward from Parliament.

Prince Edward married Duchess Victoria of Saxe-Coburg-Saalfield before the next year was out. This Victoria was a daughter of Fran Frederick Anton, a German Duke. When Edward's wife became pregnant, they were living in Germany. Prince Edward wanted his daughter to be born in England, so the pair rushed to Kensington Palace in London just before she gave birth.

A new Princess Victoria, later to become Queen Victoria, was born almost exactly a year after her mother Victoria and her husband Edward had married, on May 24, 1819, at Kensington Palace in London. Her father showered her with attention in those first months and frequently asked his wife Victoria to tell him the details of how she took care of the child.

Edward had won the race, but his happiness was short-lived. Recently, medical historians have speculated that he had been suffering from some unknown chronic condition for years, since he had been ill and often incapacitated during that time. He died of pneumonia on January 23, 1820, leaving the infant Victoria fatherless.

Victoria was born a Princess, but she was not first in the line of succession. The Prince Regent, her uncle, the Duke of York, became King when Princess Victoria's grandfather, the King, died in 1820. Another uncle, the Duke of Clarence, was still ahead of her after her grandfather and father died. George IV died in 1830. The Duke of Clarence became King William IV. William had no children; in fact, unless another child were born to one of Victoria's uncles, she would be next in line to become Sovereign. So it was that 11-year-old Princess Victoria became the heir presumptive.

# Chapter 2

# Heir Presumptive

King William IV, Victoria's uncle, did not trust her mother to act as regent if he died before the young heir presumptive officially reached adulthood at the age of 18. In fact, he was so against the Duchess that he said he was going to live until that day just to avoid her becoming Victoria's regent.

The Duchess was close friends with her comptroller, John Conroy, and they may have been lovers. These two managed Victoria's life under what became known as the Kensington System. They devised this system to control every move the young princess made, including the exact hours of her tutoring, whom she was allowed to meet, and whom she was allowed to associate with – a group that did not include many from Victoria's uncles' families.

Monitoring Victoria's daily life included imposing on her harsh moral standards. She was warned continuously to avoid sexual impropriety and admonished if the Duchess and Conroy felt that she had breached the moral code they had set in place for her. Victoria had to sleep in her mother's bedroom each night.

Victoria did have one ally, however. Her governess, Baroness Louise Lehzen, supported her against her mother, Conroy, and the Kensington System. Princess Victoria grew to admire the Baroness, who was a significant influence on her childhood. Their friendship lasted well beyond the Princess's childhood.

Victorian morality likely had origin in the Kensington System rather than in the behavior of Victoria herself. While the system was designed to keep Victoria in line and weak, the young girl could never be repressed. She was excited by the concerts and plays she attended, nature, the love of her half-sister, who was the Duchess's child by her first marriage, and all her inner desires.

Victoria wrote a story at the age of ten that revealed her melodramatic flair. Her diaries from this time and even into her adult years are filled with capital letters and exclamation points. They may have taken away her power, but they could not touch her passion.

A story is often told of the day Victoria found out she would someday be Queen. It is said that she solemnly replied: "I will be good." However, her diaries at the time that suggest that she was terrified at the prospect of being Queen. Furthermore, the Duchess kept notes regarding Victoria's behavior each day, and the word "naughty" was mentioned often.

Conroy and the Duchess took Victoria out on tours of the countryside, stopping all along the way to introduce her to the people in various towns. The tours took place in 1830 and 1832-1835. King William hated the fact that the townspeople welcomed Victoria enthusiastically and gushed over her. He felt that Conroy and the Duchess were presenting Victoria as his rival rather than his heir.

Meanwhile, Victoria spent a great deal of time with her uncle Leopold, who had become the King of the Belgians. She learned discipline from him rather than from the Kensington System. He also gave her the kind of warm attention she had missed out on when her father died.

Despite pressure from her mother to make Conroy Victoria's private secretary or at least a member of her staff, Victoria remained set against him. Not only did she manage to keep him off her staff during those years, but she banned him from seeing her when she became Queen. That day happened shortly after her uncle, King William, died on June 20, 1837.

# Chapter 3

# A Clumsy Coronation

On June 28, 1838, Queen Victoria's coronation procession followed a circular path starting at the newly completed Buckingham Palace and returning there after moving past hundreds of thousands of onlookers. It was a beautiful, sunny day, and the Queen rode in the Gold State Coach, which is still used in royal processions today. The short journey was nothing short of glorious.

However, the coronation itself was a clumsy affair saved only by the majesty of the young Queen. Benjamin Disraeli later said that the event was sorely lacking in preparation and rehearsal, and that is no doubt true.

The clergyman, Lord John Thynne, who officiated at the 5-hour-long ceremony, never seemed to know what he was supposed to do next. In fact, when talking about it later, he said that no one really knew what should happen at the coronation and so it was filled with confusion.

At one point, the Archbishop of Canterbury was supposed to deliver the Orb to Victoria. When he arrived by her side, he realized that Victoria already had it. He looked around confusedly for a few minutes and then went away.

The music contributed to the awkwardness of the ceremony, too. Music Director Sir George Smart tried to conduct the orchestra and play the organ at the same time, which did not work out very well at all. Thomas Attwood had started composing a coronation anthem before he died, but he never got the chance to complete it. The Master of the King's Music, Franz Cramer, should have written an anthem himself but failed to do so. William Knyvett finally composed an anthem, and it was played at the ceremony. But, most of the music came from Handel, including his famous "Hallelujah Chorus."

Yet, the new Queen was remarkably poised and self-confident. She had two changes of clothing during the coronation, and each gown was more luxurious than the last. It was the way Victoria behaved that set her apart from those conducting the ceremony, though. No matter what happened, she remained calm and regal.

An elderly man named Lord Rolle was to approach the throne to pay homage to Queen Victoria. As he walked up the steps, he stumbled and went rolling back down them. He kept trying and kept rolling down each time. He tried again with the crowd cheering him on, but this time, Queen Victoria handled the crisis well.

As Rolle climbed the steps toward her, she stood up from her throne and stepped down to him to prevent another tumble. The coronation audience cheered her. Artist John Martin included the mishap in his painting of the coronation, and Richard Harris Barham memorialized the occurrence in a poem, joking at Rolle's expense but praising Victoria for her queenly bearing.

When the coronation ceremony was finally over, only Queen Victoria emerged triumphantly. Soon, another ceremony would see Victoria shining in the spotlight – her marriage to Prince Albert.

# Chapter 4

# The Bedchamber Crisis

During Queen Victoria's early reign, Prime Minister Melbourne was an important father figure to her. He helped her learn about the government and helped guide her through those early years on the throne. She was very popular in the beginning, but soon afterward, the ladies of the court began to cause problems that marred her reputation.

The first crisis came in 1839 when her nemesis, John Conroy, was accused of getting one of her ladies-in-waiting pregnant. The woman's belly began to grow, and she did, indeed, look like she was with child. She despised Conroy and strongly disliked Lady Flora. Victoria believed the rumors about this Lady Flora Hastings even before she saw the evidence, but now she wanted verification.

Victoria demanded that the woman submit to a naked examination. Lady Flora at first refused.

Lady Flora eventually submitted to the exam, which revealed that she was a virgin. Conroy then led a media assault on Victoria, calling her out for believing and spreading rumors. Lady Flora died, and Victoria ordered a post mortem. To the surprise of everyone, the woman was not only not pregnant, but her body was filled with large tumors.

Whenever Victoria went out in public during that time, crowds jeered and called her "Mrs. Melbourne." Prime Minister Melbourne was so distraught over the situation that he resigned. Melbourne was a Whig. Although Victoria did not agree with the Tory agenda, she convinced a Tory, Sir Robert Peel, to create a new ministry.

Later that same year, the Bedchamber Crisis damaged Victoria's reputation even further. Peel demanded that Victoria dismiss the ladies of her bedchamber who were Whigs. Victoria flatly refused. The ladies of the bedchamber were like close friends. She would not dismiss them over politics.

Without the Queen's consent to gain the support of her Royal Household, he resigned as Prime Minister. Melbourne returned to office, much to the Queen's approval and pleasure. But,

Melbourne began to prepare her for the possibility that the next general election would prompt a change in government.

Melbourne's prediction came true when Sir Peel won the majority of the votes. He became Prime Minister. At that point, Queen Victoria had married Prince Albert. She no longer relied as much on her ladies of the bedchamber. After all, she now had Albert for company and emotional support. This time, she agreed to give Peel what he wanted. She replaced her Whig ladies with others who were Tories.

Before the end of the Bedchamber Crisis, Victoria's popularity had decreased drastically. She needed something to boost her status among the people. There was only one thing to do at that point: find a husband and marry him in a lavish ceremony. By 1840, she managed to do just that.

# Chapter 5

# Marrying Albert

Since Queen Victoria was still single, British leaders and citizens were putting pressure on her to get married and produce an heir. She was enjoying her freedom from her mother and the Kensington System too much to want to be dominated by a man. Her friend Melbourne assured her that she did not need to get married right away. Yet, she knew that she would probably get married eventually.

Her uncle Leopold was already on the case, suggesting to her that she marry his nephew Prince Albert of Saxe-Coburg-Gotha. When Victoria met him, she was utterly unimpressed. But Leopold kept pushing the idea.

Three years after their first meeting, they met again. This time, Victoria was swept off her feet. She wrote long passages in her diary about how marvelous, beautiful, handsome, and charming he was. Suddenly, her objections to getting married vanished. Five days later, on October 15, 1839, she proposed to Albert.

Albert held her hand and told her their life together would please him. That night, Victoria wrote in her diary again, this time to gush about how blessed she was to be given such a fine future husband.

Albert left in mid-November to go back to Germany for a short stay. Victoria wrote that she was sad and crying. Before he returned, she made a Declaration of Marriage before her privy councilors. Victoria was nervous about the announcement, but also ecstatic to be sharing her good news.

However, her uncle, Ernest Augustus of Hanover, opposed the marriage. He wanted to be given precedence over Albert, but Victoria settled the matter by using her Royal Prerogative to place Albert at the top of the Royal Household hierarchy, just below herself.

Albert wrote to Victoria from Germany, requesting that she make up the household from both political parties to express his political neutrality. He also wanted to have some German gentlemen at court to confide in. But Victoria flatly denied his request. From then on, it was Victoria who dominated Albert, just as others had earlier dominated her, but with one exception. She was devoted to him and cherished the time they spent together.

Albert and Victoria were married on February 10, 1840, in the Chapel Royal of St. James's Palace. Victoria wore a white dress, ornamented with beautiful lace designed by the head of the Government School of Design. The choice of a white dress was not unprecedented, but it was still rare. Women generally chose vivid colors for their wedding dresses at that time. Photography was in its infant stages, but photos were taken of the event, along with the paintings of the bride, and paintings of the wedding couple together.

Victoria wore herself out at the ceremony and spent the late evening lying down, trying to get rid of a headache. It would not be long, though, before Victoria and Albert would get together and produce the heir the country was waiting for. Victoria told Albert that they must have only a short honeymoon because she was needed as Queen of Britain. Still, she wrote passionately about their brief time alone together, a time which would set the tone for the royal sex life for the rest of Albert's life.

# Chapter 6

# Sex and Children on the Isle of Wight

Albert and Victoria had an intensely passionate love life. In fact, Victoria's sexual appetite was so overwhelming to Albert that he had a system rigged up by his bedside that allowed him to lock his doors from bed when he heard her coming. At other times, though, he would let her in, and they would have sex for hours.

Soon, Victoria was pregnant. Her first child, Victoria, Princess Royal, was born on November 21, 1840, just over nine months after their wedding day. The children followed one after another until the royal couple was parents to nine children. Albert Edward, Prince of Wales, was born on November 9, 1841; Princess Alice on April 25, 1843; Prince Alfred, Duke of Edinburgh, on August 6, 1844; Princess Helena on May 25, 1846; Princess Louise on March 18, 1848; Prince Arthur on May 1, 1850; Prince

Leopold on April 7, 1853; and Princess Beatrice on April 14, 1857.

As young lovers, the royal couple wanted to have a place where they could get away by themselves. They heard of a place on the Isle of Wight, the Osborne estate. In 1843, they began discussing the possibility of purchasing the estate. They sailed toward it through pouring rain, but just as they arrived, the sun broke through. Victoria was thoroughly enchanted and, after acquiring the property, they spent much of their time together there.

On the Isle of Wight, it was as if Albert was the monarch rather than Victoria. She learned from him and listened to his advice. She allowed him to dominate her while they were there, away from her responsibilities and away from the busy court. Yet, she felt quite differently about this domination than she had when her mother and Conroy had been in charge. She welcomed it and praised Albert to everyone who would listen.

The household bustled with the activity and happiness of all those children, but Victoria and Albert continued with their passionate love-making. They also surprised each other with nude paintings and sculptures of each other, which they placed in their estate at the Isle of Wight.

Lehzen, who had been Victoria's governess as a child, also took care of the Queen's children. Albert did not like Lehzen and felt that she caused too many problems in their family. He also blamed Lehzen for Victoria's bad moods and emotionality. But, Victoria had always been an emotional person. Certainly, the Kensington System had suppressed her passions to some degree, but her journal reveals that she was still just as prone to being overly excited, joyous, or sorrowful at every occurrence in her life.

Still, Albert wanted to get Lehzen out of the nursery. He arranged for Victoria to take a short vacation, and while she was gone, he paid Lehzen and demanded that she leave for good. Lehzen went back to Germany. Victoria saw her occasionally after Albert was gone, but they never lived in the same household again.

As for Victoria and Albert, their relationship seemed to smooth out after Lehzen's exit. Victoria let Albert know in no uncertain terms that she was the Sovereign of Britain, and he was only her husband. While she began more and more to value his opinion, it was not until members of the government appointed him to official positions that she began to respect him more. She never gave up being the head of the household, but she nearly worshipped him as a wise and valuable confidant.

Victoria, Albert, and their children attended many affairs of state, and of course, Victoria had to keep up with the nearly endless paperwork that was her duty as Queen. They spent as much time at Buckingham Palace as they needed to, to attend to these matters, but the Isle of Wight was always the home of their hearts.

The fact that Victoria loved Albert with an indescribable intensity is revealed in her many diaries. She also loved his ideas and plans. In 1851, she would be present to see the results of one of his most ambitious undertakings.

# Chapter 7

# The Crystal Palace Exhibition

Prince Albert and other members of the Royal Society for the Encouragement of Arts, Manufactures, and Commerce planned for a grand 6-month event during 1851. It was called the Great Exhibition of the Works of Industry of All Nations, or, more commonly, the Great Exhibition. Some called it the Crystal Palace Exhibition, referring to a magnificent glass building at the center of the exhibition grounds. Although the Queen herself did not participate directly in its planning, it was closely associated with her reign.

The time before the Great Exhibition had been turbulent across Europe. The British leaders, including Queen Victoria, wanted Britain to stand out as the most powerful and most technologically advanced of all the other countries and empires. The Royal Society's answer was to gather leaders in technology from around the world in one place where Britain's superiority could be demonstrated.

Albert promoted the event even before the Royal Commission for the Exhibition of 1851 was formed to look into the viability of hosting the event. He continued to give his political support to the Exhibition as the grounds, including the Crystal Palace, were designed and built. He attended the event often, and Queen Victoria and her family were present three times between the start of the exhibition on May 1, 1851, and its close on October 22, 1851.

The opening of the event was glorious. The Queen's procession at the event featured continuous live music from organs that were being exhibited at the exposition. The atmosphere was like a joyous party, despite the Conservatives' fears that the crowd would turn into a revolutionary mob. Some even opposed the Queen's attendance at the event, suggesting she should stay out of harm's way on the Isle of Wight. But, the Queen would not be deterred. She wanted to be a part of the event that her husband had planned.

Some of the exhibitions were working examples of industry. For example, one included the manufacture of cloth from spinning the thread to making the cloth, creating finished products that were then sold at the fair. Some of the new technological achievements presented at the fair included the telegraph, vulcanized rubber, and new surgical instruments.

The Great Exhibition was the first of many World's Fairs. Over six million people attended it in all, and it raised money for the Victoria and Albert Museum, the Science Museum, and the Natural History Museum. Extra money from its proceeds was set aside in a trust to provide scholarships and grants for industrial research.

Many famous people attended the event, including writers Lewis Carroll, Alfred Tennyson, Charlotte Bronte, Charles Dickens, George Eliot; scientists such as Charles Darwin; manufacturers such as Samuel Colt; and members of various Royal Families from around Europe. The Great Exhibition was Prince Albert's crowning achievement and generated a significant boost in the Queen's popularity. Queen Victoria was thrilled about the success of the event. Ten years later, her happy time with Albert would come to a cruel end.

# Chapter 8

## Widowhood and Seclusion

While living at the Osborne House on the Isle of Wight, Queen Victoria vowed that no matter what happened, she would follow Albert's advice. She said she would do things the way he wanted her to do them for the rest of her life. Unfortunately, she would soon have to guess what he wanted her to do. He would no longer be available to guide her as a wife, mother, and Queen. Albert departed from her forever on December 14, 1861, and Victoria would never be the same again.

Albert had suffered from stomach problems for years, but in 1861, his illness became more serious. Despite being ill, he still assisted Victoria in many different ways. He also took a trip to confront his son, the Prince of Wales, because it was rumored that he had slept with an Irish actress. By December of that year, he was gravely ill. His doctor diagnosed his illness as typhoid fever. He died on December 14, 1861.

Victoria, devastated, blamed her son's promiscuity for Albert's sickness and death. She was so distraught that she went into seclusion and took to wearing black, a habit which she continued for the rest of her life. She missed Albert so much that she slept with a plaster cast of his head beside her in her bed. She also kept his room the same as when he died until she died herself. She kept all his things scattered around the large house, just as he had left them. He was gone, but never forgotten.

Victoria's joyous demeanor evaporated. She now looked at the world with sadness, bitterness, and cynicism. People began to call her "The Widow of Windsor" because that became the entire focus of her life. She still had a sense of humor, although it became less openhearted and more sarcastic.

She is often credited with the quote, "We are not amused." As the story goes, someone attending dinner with her at Windsor Castle told a story about a scandal that was taking place at the time. He told it in the hopes of bringing a bit of lively conversation and interest into the sad house. But Victoria supposedly shut him down immediately when she said those four magic words. There is little evidence to support that she actually said it, and in later years, she told people that she had never said it. However, one historian suggests that she probably did say it, but as an ironic joke.

Queen Victoria did keep up with her official duties, but she managed to take care of them mostly from her three residences at Osborne House, Windsor Castle and Balmoral Castle, the latter of which she and Albert had acquired shortly before his death. At one point, a notice was posted on Buckingham Palace, saying that it would be closed due to her "declining business." On the advice of her old friend Melbourne, she began appearing in public again, although on a limited basis.

In 1866, Queen Victoria went to the State Opening of Parliament, and the next year, she supported passing the Reform Act of 1867, which gave voting privileges to urban men. However, she remained against giving women the right to vote.

Since the Queen was mostly absent from political discussions and government meetings, the government began to move towards republicanism. Protesters arrived in Trafalgar Square to demand Victoria's removal, but she was not about to leave. When her son got typhoid fever, she was worried that he would die young, as his father had. When he survived and got well again, Queen Victoria and her children attended a parade in London to commemorate his recovery. The event made her more popular again, and the calls for her removal slowly faded away. Victoria returned to public life, but this time on a more limited basis. She felt above all that the Queen should present a solemn and stable bearing. A straitlaced and dignified demeanor replaced her emotionality. She was Queen, after all, and the love of her life was gone forever. She was more than ready to behave like a grown ruler in the way that she imagined one should act.

Yet, Victoria still had a love relationship ahead of her. She had grown fond of her Scottish servant, John Brown. The rumors of their passionate affair shocked the people of her time and have confounded historians ever since.

# Chapter 9

# John Brown: Victoria's Secret Husband?

With her dear Albert gone, Queen Victoria seemed a dour and dismal woman. At the age of 42, she was alone. Or was she? During the 1860s, she began appearing in public with her Scottish servant, John Brown. She was often derisively called "Mrs. Brown" by both courtiers and schoolchildren. Others called Brown "the Queen's stallion," and her own children called him "Mama's lover." Some even suggested that Brown and Victoria had secretly married at Crathie Kirk, the small church attended by Royal Families through the years while they were residing at Balmoral Castle in Scotland. A priest even confessed on his deathbed that he had performed the marriage ceremony.

Yet, questions still remain for many historians. If they were indeed married, why are there no records? Why was the government not informed? Where is the concrete evidence that such a marriage or even an intimate friendship existed? Certainly they spent a great deal of time together, but where are the letters and diary entries that Victoria would undoubtedly have written about him?

The marriage may have been an informal pledge of commitment to their already deep friendship rather than a ceremony to mark the beginning of a true marriage. Brown was always there for him, and Victoria did mention to her friends that he was more devoted to her than anyone else. They spent many hours roaming the Scottish highlands, where he carried her across muddy roads. Then, after Albert's death, Victoria had him reassigned to watch over her at the Osborne House on the Isle of Wight.

So, where are the diaries and letters? They no longer exist, but there is good evidence that they once did. After Victoria's death, her daughter Beatrice edited her diaries and removed anything she deemed improper. There were some 300 hundred letters that were being used as blackmail against Victoria's son Edward VII. Sir James Reid, Victoria's doctor for 20 years before her death, was sent to negotiate the return of the letters, and they were destroyed immediately. Sir James must have read the letters because he said that they were very compromising.

Victoria also began writing a memoir about John Brown's life. However, she was persuaded to abandon the project, and the part she had already completed was destroyed. She did publish a book, though, titled *Leaves of the Journal of Our Life in the Highlands* in which she talked about him and praised him.

Sir James's own records were also destroyed, but his notes about the records remain. One of the notes describes an incident in which John Brown was present when Victoria was getting ready to have a physical examination. He lifted up his kilt and said, "There it is!" to which Victoria responded by lifting her skirt and saying, "No, here it is!"

This incident reveals something about their relationship, but it is hard to know the exact nature of the exchange. They could have been flirting with each other, although that would have been deemed highly inappropriate for a woman of the Queen's stature and a lowly servant. Even if it had somehow been a friendly joke, it would have gone far beyond the boundaries of decency in Victorian Britain. At that time, it was scandalous to even show a leg to a member of the opposite sex without the benefit of marriage.

A sculptor, Edgar Boehm, had seen the couple up close and told the story that Victoria allowed him all the privileges of marriage. Several biographers and historians have said that the relationship was platonic, but it seems unlikely in view of their behavior in front of the doctor. Brown's diaries were also destroyed, which can easily lead to the conclusion that there was something in them that the Royal children did not want to be made public.

Victoria told her sister-in-law that his was the "truest heart that ever beat." Victoria and John slept together each night, but it is unclear whether they consummated their relationship or simply enjoyed the closeness and comfort they found in each other's arms. The truth of the matter is that, whatever else might be said of Victoria's relationship with Brown, she did love him. When he died, she grieved him more deeply than anyone else she had lost except for Albert.

Brown was Victoria's confidante, her greatest supporter, her escort to public events, her protector, and yes, her friend. And, Brown would have many opportunities to protect her, as he defended her from several physical attacks that happened after she lost Albert.

# Chapter 10

# Assassination Attempts and Attacks

The assassination attempts on Victoria's life began early in her reign, the same year she married Albert. Some shot at her, while others simply attacked her. Through it all, she remained her regal self and relied on others to handle the crises.

In 1840, the Queen was riding through London in her carriage. Edward Oxford, an 18-year-old, walked up to the carriage and fired two shots at her. He was accused of high treason but got off on an insanity plea. This angered Victoria, who wanted him to be punished severely.

Another man, named John Francis, tried to shoot the Queen in her carriage in 1842. He tried, not once, but twice and was unsuccessful both times. He missed with the first shot. The second time, the police were ready for him, captured him, and took him in. He was found guilty of high treason. He was sentenced to execution, but his sentence was commuted, and he was sent to the penal colony in Australia.

Also, in 1842, a somewhat silly attempt was made on her life. This time, it was William Bean who made an attempt. However, he apparently did not have the proper ammunition. Instead, he filled the pistol with paper and tobacco. He did 18 months in jail for his indiscretion.

Victoria seemed to be most vulnerable to these attacks while riding in her carriage. In 1849, William Hamilton, who was described as "an angry Irishman," fired at her. Then, Robert Pane, an ex-Army officer, decided to forgo the usual weapon. He rushed up to her carriage and started beating her with his cane.

Being with Albert may have added to the Queen's vulnerability, too. He was a bit of a weakling and liked to stay out of physical conflicts. In fact, when Victoria first met him, she described him as an invalid, referring to his frailty and timid disposition. But when John Brown began to accompany Queen Victoria, things changed. He was more than six feet tall, muscular, and ready to take on any attacker. His attitude alone may have been enough to deter attacks on his companion, the Queen.

In 1872, another Irishman, this one named Arthur O'Connell, came at Victoria's carriage, holding a gun and a petition to free Irish prisoners. John Brown pushed him to the ground before the Queen even knew what was happening. Brown won a gold medal for his act of bravery.

Other would-be assassins claimed to have made attempts on the queen's life, whether they confessed because they had a guilty conscience or simply wanted attention. One of these said he had tried eight times to kill the Queen. On the eighth try, in 1882, he shot at her in her carriage as it was leaving the train station. This was the Scottish poet Roderick Maclean, who was declared insane and forced to spend the rest of his life in an asylum. Queen Victoria was so frustrated by Maclean's verdict of "not guilty but insane" that she encouraged Parliament to create a new type of verdict – "guilty, but insane."

Although Victoria found these attempts and attacks distressing and most disrespectful, she did have one benefit from each of them. Every time someone threatened to do bodily harm to the Queen, her popularity soared.

# Chapter 11

# Religious Dissenter, Social Changer, Philanthropist

Queen Victoria had very specific ideas about how the world should work, and she was straightforward about expressing them and pursuing her goals. And, over the course of her reign, life did change in Britain, and mostly for the better.

Victoria, as Queen of the U.K., was the official head of the Church of England. However, Queen Victoria confided that
 she was more of a Presbyterian at heart, and nearly a religious dissenter. She much preferred the Scottish Presbyterian Church, which she regularly attended whenever she stayed at Balmoral Castle in Scotland. She felt that the Church of England should be further reformed to make it more strictly Protestant. At the same time, Methodist and Baptist denominations flourished throughout the U.K.

Religion was a significant part of life for nearly everyone during Victoria's reign. Even the prison walls bore Christian messages for the prisoners. Religious symbols were everywhere. Victoria, along with the majority of the British people, believed it was Britain's job to save the world. Missionary projects were started or expanded during this time.

Victoria also believed that those born into royalty had a duty to public service. Albert agreed with her. In fact, he told their son that he should carry out his Christian duties cheerfully if he wanted to be deemed a true gentleman. With hard work, modesty, honesty, and philanthropy as the main themes of her Calvinist religious philosophy, Victoria felt it was her duty to help the poor and unfortunate, as long as they were worthy of help.

The Queen not only helped others on a personal level, but she also signed into law many of the social welfare reforms that made life easier for the common people. These included free education, reasonable working hours and conditions, and improved health care. Victoria believed the world could be united and that peace could be achieved by means of constitutional monarchies. She signed legislation making Britain's government more democratic and hoped that her son-in-law, Emperor Frederick III of Germany would follow her lead in becoming a constitutional monarch.

Queen Victoria's views on equal rights for women went along with the way she was raised. Although she believed men and women were equal, she abhorred feminism because she worried that feminists would lead women away from morality. In fact, she said feminists deserved a "good whipping."

On the other hand, she dedicated herself to seeing that the Jewish people were treated fairly. The first Jews to serve in Parliament and the first Jewish Lord Mayor of London took office during her reign. Her favorite prime minister, Benjamin Disraeli, was the first Jewish prime minister to take office in the U.K. Of all the prime ministers during her time on the throne, Prime Minister Disraeli had the best working relationship with the Queen.

# Chapter 12

# Disraeli and Gladstone

From the beginning of Queen Victoria's reign until her death, nine different prime ministers held office. She had found a fatherly figure and helpful counselor in her first, Prime Minister Melbourne. She liked some of them more than others, but her favorite was Benjamin Disraeli, who was opposed by William Ewart Gladstone on almost every issue.

Disraeli took office in 1868 and immediately won the Queen's favor, charming her with praise and flattery. Disraeli had little time to make changes in the British government as his time in office only lasted a few short months. He was replaced by Gladstone, who spoke to her in a cold, informal way – much differently than Disraeli, who had talked to her more as a woman than a ruler.

The Queen was still in seclusion following Albert's death when Gladstone took office.  At a

Republican rally in Trafalgar Square, protestors demanded her removal from the government. To counter what she believed were Gladstone's faulty policies, she began to put aside mourning and rejoin British society in the 1870s. She attended parades and church services and took a more active role in the government.

In the election of 1874, Gladstone was defeated, and Disraeli became prime minister again. Queen Victoria, of course, was pleased just to see him back in office. But Disraeli made her even happier when he pushed for the Royal Titles Act of 1876. He also passed the Public Worship Regulation Act of 1874, which eliminated Catholic rituals for services in the Church of England, a change Victoria had wanted for years.

This Act of Parliament gave Victoria the title of Empress of India. Having an additional title of Empress was important at that time. Without it, her daughter Victoria, Princess Royal, would have eventually outranked her with an Empress title of her own once her husband, the heir to the German Empire, became Emperor. She was so pleased with Disraeli that she made him Earl of Beaconsfield.

Unfortunately for the Queen, Disraeli's administration failed to carry the vote in 1880. The Queen tried to convince Lord Harrington, who was at that time leader of the Liberals, to serve as Prime Minister. However, Harrington declined, saying a Liberal government could only succeed with Gladstone at its helm. Victoria reluctantly appointed Gladstone as the prime minister.

Before Gladstone's government fell in 1885, he had proposed and pushed the passage of the Representation of the People Act of 1884, increasing the electorate far beyond what Victoria found reasonable. A Conservative, Robert Gascoyne-Cecil, became the new prime minister, but his power was short-lived. Gladstone returned to serve as Prime Minister again the following year.

This time, Gladstone made a fatal mistake. He introduced the Irish Home Rule Bill, which would give Ireland a separate legislature. Victoria was against the bill, and so was the House of Commons. When the bill was rejected, Gladstone resigned.

Gladstone was Prime Minister again in 1892, much to the Queen's dismay. He tried for another Irish Home Rule Bill. When the measure was again defeated, Gladstone retired from political life.

# Chapter 13

# Foreign Affairs

Victoria was Queen of so many different lands during her reign that it was said that the sun never set on the British Empire. She took pride in the U.K. and all its colonies and territories and enjoyed being their Queen. As the first of the modern British monarchs, Queen Victoria limited her role in government to offering her encouragement, advice on the issues of the day, and warnings of possible conflicts.

Victoria relished her title of Empress of India. She was a benevolent Queen to the Indian people, offering generous encouragement to the people in the proclamation that declared India a part of the British Empire. Although a devout Christian herself, Victoria believed that others should be allowed to follow their own consciences. She encouraged the British government to give the people of India religious freedom and uphold their right to worship in their own way.

When Disraeli was Prime Minister, he advocated an expansionist foreign policy. Queen Victoria agreed with this because she felt that being a part of the British Empire would bring stability and civilization. She saw British rule as the best alternative for countries that were vulnerable to being taken over by tyrants. She also wanted Britain to be the most powerful country in the world. Yet, she did not want to annex countries unless she felt forced by circumstances to do so.

Queen Victoria tried to exert her power to create the British Empire she envisioned and maintain world order. From April 1877 to February 1878, she pushed Disraeli to get involved in the Russo-Turkish War. She even went so far as threatening to abdicate the throne if Disraeli did not follow her wishes. However, in this instance, Victoria could do little to change the course of history. With the signing of the Treaty of Berlin, the war was over without Victoria having any effect on it at all.

Toward the end of Victoria's reign, the Second Boer War was going on in South Africa. Victoria supported the involvement of the U.K. in the crisis but was suffering so many tragedies at the time that she gave it little attention.

The Queen visited many European countries during her reign. She was the first British monarch ever to go to Spain and the first to visit France since Henry VIII went there in 1520.

While in France, she stayed on the French Riviera. In an uncharacteristic move, Queen Victoria allowed Sarah Bernhardt to perform for her, which dispelled the myth that the Queen could only entertainments that followed an overly strict moral theme. And, it was not surprising that she enjoyed the show since she had been going to see plays, concerts and art exhibits since she was a young girl.

Until Victoria began visiting the French Riviera, it had been mainly associated with convalescence. After Victoria went there, again and again, it became a holiday center and one of the most popular tourist spots in Europe.

Queen Victoria had her informal intelligence service in France. She had many cousins widely scattered around Europe. She wrote letters to them to find out what was happening in their countries, where many of them held high positions. This allowed her to give helpful advice and warnings to her Prime Ministers.

Victoria's last major tour outside England was a trip to Ireland. While there, she was often greeted by protestors. But, she still managed to charm most of the Irish people with her inspiring messages of hope and peace.

Albert was from Germany, so it was natural that the couple made several trips to that country. The first time, they stayed in Rosenau, a small castle north-east of Coburg, Albert's birthplace. Coburg was her favorite place to live. In fact, she loved it so much that Disraeli felt it necessary to advise her that she could not rule Britain from Coburg. Late in life, she even said that if she were not Queen, she would like to spend the rest of her life there.

Still, she had a life in the U.K. and many enjoyable times ahead of her. She had to be at home in Britain to join in the lavish nationwide parties held for her Gold and Diamond Jubilees.

# Chapter 14

# Queenly Celebrations and the Jubilee Plot

On June 20, 1887, Queen Victoria and the entire British Empire celebrated her 50th year as Queen. This Golden Jubilee was a spectacular event both at home in the U.K. and in the many British colonies. Fifty Kings and Queens from around the world and their escorts were invited to Buckingham Palace to join in the festivities.

The Queen had helped plan the celebration, insisting that the event focus on Victoria as a mother figure. Her children had grown up, and some of them were world leaders in their own rights or as partners of royal spouses. Victoria became known as the Grandmother of Europe. She also wanted to express her motherly feelings towards her colonies, particularly India.

Rather than wearing a crown for the occasion, Victoria chose to wear a bonnet, and she advised that other women should do the same. But, while Victoria was planning her Jubilee, a group of Irish nationals was plotting to create havoc at that very festival.

The Jubilee Plot was not discovered until October 1887, when British police found bombs hidden away in Westminster Abbey. Although it was rumored that the plot originated in the British government, the investigation only revealed an American and two Irishmen as leaders of the failed assassination attempt.

The Golden Jubilee opened with a breakfast at Windsor Castle, followed by a carriage ride through roaring crowds on the way to Windsor Station. The Royal Family traveled by train to London, where they were greeted again by cheering crowds as they made their way to Buckingham Palace for a luncheon feast. The night's activities included a magnificent dinner with the 50 royal guests who had been invited. They ate on gold plates and joined in a conversation that lasted well into the evening.

The next day, the Queen attended a special thanksgiving service at Westminster Abbey, but the Jubilee Plot had fizzled out by then, and the service went off without any problems.

Just after her Golden Jubilee, Victoria began taking Hindu lessons from an Indian named Abdul Karim. The two became very close, and many people in Britain likened their relationship to the one the Queen had shared with John Brown. Some members of the British government believed that Victoria's Munshi, or teacher, was a threat to national security. Many opposed him, and even Victoria's son Edward VII, who succeeded her to the throne, refused to acknowledge him. Edward burnt most of the letters Victoria exchanged with her Indian teacher.

Not long before Victoria's Diamond Jubilee, which celebrated her 60th year as Queen, the Jamison Raid in South Africa created a hostile situation that led to the Boer War. To make matters worse, Kaiser Wilhelm, who was Victoria's grandson, sent a message to the South African Boer leader to congratulate him for defeating the British in Raid.

On September 23, 1896, Victoria reached another milestone in her reign as she became the longest-reigning monarch in the history of England, Scotland, and Britain. She wanted to celebrate but suggested the event be moved to June 1897 to coincide with her Diamond Jubilee.

Victoria was now an old woman. Her Diamond Jubilee had to take her fragile condition into account in many respects. Rather than going inside Westminster Abbey for a formal thanksgiving service, her carriage merely stopped at the steps of St. Paul's Cathedral for a few words of thanksgiving for her prosperity and success as Queen and the stability of the British Empire. With her reign nearly at an end, Victoria celebrated once again with European royalty.

# Chapter 15

# Confusion, Death, and Legacy

Queen Victoria had lived her life with intelligence, passion, and a strict moral code. When 1900 arrived, it brought her so many family tragedies that she called it her most "horrid year." She had lived a long life, but she had children and grandchildren who were not so lucky. That year was also a difficult one for her because of her work to keep the national press on track as it reported on the Boer War.

Victoria was in a wheelchair and had failing eyesight, although she refused to wear her spectacles in public. She considered them not only unattractive but also not in fitting with her royal image. When she attended the Irish Industries Exhibition that year, it was the last time she was seen alive in public.

In December, Victoria's health began to slip even further. By January 14, 19o1, she was riding in a carriage with her deceased son's widow, confused and unaware of her surroundings. On January 16, her doctor released the information that she was ill. During the next days, she would get better for a time and then worse still. She died on January 22, 1901, surrounded by the surviving members of her family.

Victoria had made funeral plans for herself, and her family carried them out respectfully. She was dressed in white, and her wedding veil was placed on her head. Her coffin was also white. Rings that Albert had given her were placed on her hand. A plaster cast of Albert's hand was placed in hers.

Queen Victoria had also secretly given instructions that a ring John Brown had given her be placed on her finger and a lock of Brown's hair placed in her hand. Both of her wishes were carried out, despite the family's earlier disapproval of him.

There were no black horses or black draperies at Queen Victoria's funeral. She wanted a white funeral, and that is what she got. At the end of the services, her casket was brought to the Frogmore Mausoleum and laid beside Albert's.

The country and indeed the entire British Empire mourned the loss of the only British queen that had ruled during most of their lifetimes. The Queen had left a legacy of stability for the U.K., empowerment of the Indian race, and improved conditions for the people of her country. Many historians put her on a short list of the greatest British monarchs.

Unfortunately, Victoria left another legacy for her family. She was the first known carrier of hemophilia. Women carry the disease, and those affected by it are usually men. As her children and grandchildren spread out across Europe, the disease entered the bloodlines of those countries' royalty. The good news is that the type of hemophilia that Queen Victoria passed on to her children, type B, is now thought to be extinct.

When the grieving for Victoria came to an end, a new era dawned in Britain. Strict morality was replaced with freer ideas of what was right and good. Yet, the Victorian Era has remained an important part of the character of the British monarchy. It may be hard for people in the 21st century to understand Victorian mores and attitudes, but the progress that happened during her reign is hard to refute.

# Chapter 16

# The Victorian Era

Very soon after Queen Victoria died, the fashions, hairstyles, and mores of her time were seen as old-fashioned and out-of-date. When someone or something was called "Victorian," it was considered an insult. This distaste for all things Victorian continued for about 20 years until a biographer published the story of her life in 1921.

Soon, Victorian goods and fashions were interesting again. Antique stores started selling more and more Victorian furniture, knickknacks, and souvenirs. In the years since the 1920s, Victorian fashions have moved in and out of favor in Britain and the world. Victorian ideals are largely a thing of the past, and most people would still bristle if they were described as having a Victorian attitude.

The Victorian years were mostly happy ones for the British people. It was a time of peace, prosperity, and stability. A robust middle class developed in Britain, with privacy and domesticity as its central themes. Employers gave working-class people better lives as social welfare became a bigger priority. Yet, taxes were low during the entire period.

People were earning more, but spending less time at work. With more time on their hands, people began taking advantage of more opportunities to participate in leisure activities. First, the white-collar workers and then the working class began to take yearly vacations. Religious restrictions against secular activities on Sundays were relaxed, giving people another day to enjoy recreational activities. Sporting events, music hall concerts, dances, and popular theater gave people even more ways to play.

Men in the Victorian Era often went to gentlemen's dining clubs, such as The Beefsteak Club or the Savage Club, or spent an evening gambling in one of the many small casinos. Women could now participate in some sports, including badminton and archery. Women also gathered at one another's homes for teas and luncheons.

The arts flourished during the Victorian Age. Gothic Revival architecture became the norm for new and important buildings. Photography became increasingly popular, and Victoria was the first British monarch to have her photo taken. Photography also influenced many artists during the time, including John Everett Millais and other Pre-Raphaelite artists. During the later years of the period, Impressionism and Social Realism techniques would dominate the arts in Britain.

Journalism expanded its reach due to better transportation and, of course, better printing presses. *The Times*, London's newspaper, was the first to send out war correspondents to cover conflicts abroad. Better reporting led to social reforms, including the advancement of nursing techniques led by Florence Nightingale.

Britain was the center of the industrialized world at the time. The people believed that technology would improve the world, so they supported science wholeheartedly. British engineers were at the top of their profession, designing and building railroads, improving industrial processes, and contributing to the tools available to many other professions.

Were there any social problems at all during the Victorian Era? Of course. It was a notorious time for cruel child labor practices in the U.K. A rapidly increasing population led to more poverty in urban areas, where many people lived in slum housing. Prostitution was a major social problem, too, with as many as 8,600 prostitutes working the streets of London in 1857 alone.

Yet, despite the problems of the time, the Victorian Era was a gentler time for most British citizens. Queen Victoria herself did everything she could to create a better world for her people and all the people of the world. She was ahead of her time in speaking out against racial prejudice. She saw the beginnings of many varieties of social reform. She may have left many improvements still to be made when she died, but so has any ruler who has ever lived.

# Conclusion

Queen Victoria was one of the most influential people of the 19th century. She presented herself to the public as a serious-minded and proper lady, but in private and in her diaries, she revealed her passionate love for those she held dear and her fiery temper for those who crossed her.

Victoria's marriage to Albert was one of the greatest love affairs of all time. Victoria did not believe in remarriage, so there was no new consort after Albert died. Yet, she was known to flirt with men she trusted, and she had at least one grand love affair after Albert's death.

When one considers the length of her life and her reign, it is not surprising that Victoria's views changed over the years. Her character diminished and then softened as she neared death. When she was gone, the country moved on very quickly to the next new thing. But during the time that Victoria was Queen, the British people were her greatest allies.

Made in the USA
Coppell, TX
05 May 2020